WHITES

Also by Otegha Uwagba

Little Black Book

WHITES

ON RACE AND OTHER FALSEHOODS

OTEGHA UWAGBA

4th Estate • London

4th Estate
An imprint of HarperCollins*Publishers*
1 London Bridge Street
London SE1 9GF

www.4thEstate.co.uk

First published in Great Britain in 2020 by 4th Estate

1

A catalogue record for this book is available from the British Library

ISBN 978-0-00-844042-8 (paperback)

Printed and bound in CPI Group (UK) Ltd, Croydon

MIX
Paper from
responsible sources
FSC™ C007454

This book is produced from independently certified FSC paper
to ensure responsible forest management

Find out more about HarperCollins and the environment at
www.harpercollins.co.uk/green

'To know our whites is to understand the psychology of white people and the elasticity of whiteness. It is to be intimate with some white persons but to critically withhold faith in white people categorically.'

Dr Tressie McMillan Cottom, *Thick*

PREAMBLE

This essay was written in the throes of an unthinkable summer, one where it seemed as though the entire world was teetering on the brink of collapse, and where I often imagined I could physically *feel* the shift from one era to another happening beneath my feet, could actually point at the fault line separating one period of time from the next and say, 'There. That's where it happened.'

And then, in the middle of that already strange season, George Floyd, a 46-year-old Black American man from Fayetteville, North Carolina, was killed by a white police officer – a death that Floyd's brother would later describe as a 'modern-day lynching' – and the world burst into flames.

The days and weeks that followed brought to a head countless tensions and unspoken grievances, at both the civic and personal levels, and it was the ripple effect of those events that prompted me to finally begin writing this essay. The thoughts that follow are largely constructed from notes I started making around five years ago: a collection of miscellaneous observations and emotions piling up day by day, lost memories abruptly making themselves known again and taking on new significance when arranged on a shelf alongside twenty others.

Sifting through them, a very clear unifying theme quickly became obvious: not just 'racism' in a general sense – which is what I had thought I was writing about – but white people, and what is required to coexist with them if you yourself are not white. The colossal burden of that requirement.

Already, my first hurdle: I didn't particularly want to write an essay about being Black that placed white people at its centre. I felt – still feel – deeply confronted by that prospect, wary of falling into the easy trap of evaluating Black experiences solely in relation to whiteness. As I weighed this up, an interview with the New York-based artist Rashid Johnson caught my eye. Part of a larger feature focusing on contemporary Black artists actively resisting the expectation to create work catering to the white gaze (as is often the unspoken mandate in creative fields),[1] Johnson noted that society consistently finds new ways 'to position the work of Black artists as inherently being in response to the obstacles presented by a white world.' That was the very opposite of what I wanted to do – produce something angled toward the white gaze, or write an essay that might become an emblem for progressive white people wanting to prove their credentials, wallowing in their guilt about the existence of a system that works to their advantage while doing nothing to divest from it.

All this to say that although I didn't want to write an essay where white people took centre stage, as you'll discover, that's exactly what I've done. This essay is very much 'a response to the obstacles presented by a white world'. It became clear to me that to write about navigating racism and *not* place white people at the centre of that narrative would be to elide the very thing I was trying to write about, because navigating racism is really a matter of navigating white people.

Perhaps that conclusion seems obvious, but it took me a little while to get there, and to work through my competing desires about how to approach this essay. On reflection, that push and pull – between what I wanted to do, and what racism necessarily requires of me – seems strangely apt, a facsimile of whiteness itself and the way it compels, overrides, distorts, and ultimately controls.

I still haven't watched George Floyd die.

I've seen stills from *that* video embedded into news articles, and when I'm scrolling through social media I'll occasionally stumble across a few seconds of his ordeal if a video clip unexpectedly begins to autoplay, but I haven't watched the video that so many found themselves watching at the start of this summer. I haven't watched a grown man undone by the knowledge of his impending death, pleading alternately for two life-giving forces, for his mother and for air. I haven't witnessed the precise moment where he passes from living to dead, the last few dregs of life gurgling out of him, squeezed out beneath the heft of someone else's knee.

Mostly this is because I already made that mistake a few months earlier, with Ahmaud Arbery. Shocked by what I'd read about his murder, but unable to wrap my head around the idea that such an egregiously violent act had somehow gone unpunished, I felt compelled to see it with my own eyes, even in my guilt at stripping this man of his last shred of dignity by gawping at the spectacle of his death. The video I found played itself on an endless loop, so I watched it again and again and again and again, committing every second to memory, trying to understand. His baggy white T-shirt, and loose running shorts. The off-screen tussle over a shotgun, and the sharp pop of gunfire before Arbery emerges back into frame, loping languidly across the street. At first it looks like he is breaking into a jog, about to resume his run, the situation resolved. But then a red stain blooms across his T-shirt and seconds later he collapses to the ground, limbs suddenly liquid. And then he's dead.

I watched that sordid video enough times, can picture it so clearly in my mind's eye even all these months later, that I knew I didn't want to go through the same thing with George Floyd. I don't want to accept that he's dead, and that he died the way he did, so I keep skipping over that part of his story and the abject horror of those final eight minutes and forty-six seconds.

I've watched other videos of him though, videos from when he was still alive. It feels trite to say it but that's how I feel he deserves to be remembered, how *I* want to remember him. A short snippet of him rapping (for a while Floyd was part of Houston's chopped and screwed music scene, performing under the name Big Floyd). Another video in which he is offering motivational life advice, hinting at his own past struggles and urging resilience in the face of adversity, announcing in his gloopy southern drawl, 'man, I love the world!' The stories that have since emerged about his life from family and friends, and from his widowed fiancée, confirm that yes, George Floyd certainly did love the world, even if ultimately it didn't love him back.

In the aftermath of his death came the truly unexpected: a prolonged and visceral, full-throated outpouring of rage, of global protests and riots and emotionally charged op-eds, demanding justice and prosecutions and change. The stuff that history books are made of, I thought, as I watched it all unfold, and in fact I have never before been so keenly aware that I am watching history being writ-ten. 'Watching' being the operative word here, because I was not 'in it' – not in the USA, the beating heart of the movement, nor out on the streets here in Britain, having decided that my responsibility not to risk passing the virus on to the loved ones I was isolating with outweighed my desire to protest. I experienced it all at a remove, filtered through the often opposing lenses of social and mass media – though even from that vantage point there was still plenty to see.

That George Floyd's death would command so much attention is in some ways deeply surprising, given that it happened to coincide with our collectively being trapped in the horror of a global pandemic. Amid scenes that had the nightmarish, alt-reality quality of a Jordan Peele movie – masks, mass graves and growing piles of bodies, armed militias, sudden and incomprehensible, almost *random* death – one wonders how the unlawful killing of one Black man, when there have been so many, managed to cut through the noise, how George Floyd was not merely a tree falling unobserved in a forest.

But then as with Peele's films, the nature and distribution of those deaths offered potent commentary on the ravages of structural racism, as evidence began to emerge that, certainly within Britain and the USA (whose governments seemed to be competing to top the global league table of pandemic-related deaths), people of colour were dying from the virus at disproportionately high rates. At the same time the underpaid 'key workers' upon whom we were now more dependent than ever – again disproportionately people of colour – had become the battering ram that those governments were using to absorb the impact of the virus, hell-bent on keeping the engines of commerce churning at all costs, even when that cost was the loss of human life. Meanwhile, giant swathes of the population who had already been clinging on by their fingertips were sent careening into financial free-fall. Floyd himself had lost his job as a security guard at a bar and restaurant affected by the pandemic-related shutdown, contracting coronavirus just weeks before his death. One pandemic had simply worsened another, the virus simultaneously highlighting and exacerbating the racial inequalities that had put George Floyd in a situation where someone might feel emboldened enough to murder him in broad daylight, in full knowledge that their actions were being captured on camera.

Cut off from friends and family, without the usual trivialities to distract and comfort and sometimes only the endless scroll of the Internet for company, we were a captive audience, an already raw nerve primed to absorb the sheer wickedness of what had happened to this man. Our phones stood poised to deliver on-demand horror at any time of day or night, whenever we summoned it in fact (which judging from my own experiences, was often). Combine all this with a population already furious at the almost criminally incompetent politicians charged with protecting us, and on high alert for injustice of any kind, George Floyd's murder would be the kerosene on an already volatile situation, igniting an unprecedented reckoning that extended far beyond the frequently lethal bias of the criminal justice system, abruptly ripping back the bedcovers from the many systems and institutions that have anti-Blackness at their core.

Perhaps the most unusual thing in this season of already excessively unusual things was the depth of white support that emerged in response to George Floyd's murder. Both his death and the subsequent scrutiny of institutional racism completely co-opted the news cycle, breaking out of the Black community (where it would always have been a big deal) to dominate the white mainstream as well. Images of protestors that circulated across news channels and social media made it clear that there were nearly as many white protestors as Black ones, and all over the world white people rushed to condemn, to support and to affirm their commitments to racial equality.

The obvious logic would have me gratified by these responses, satisfied that at last a critical mass of white people were up in arms about racism and acknowledging their own complicity. And yet I can only describe my reaction as that of a barely suppressed eye-roll and admit that I felt deeply unmoved by much of it. Watching so many white people grapple with the reality of racism for the very first time, I could think only of the fact that white people were grappling with the reality of racism *for the very first time*. This sudden concern over racial injustice felt too long overdue, and I resented the choices that had allowed them to remain so oblivious for so long. After all, Black people are not born with an innate understanding of racism. We have to learn about it along the way, so it's galling to realise that its main perpetrators and beneficiaries have not fully grasped its inner workings, that they are not in fact *intimately* familiar with it. That kind of ignorance, to me, feels wilful.

And, as conversations about the circumstances and climate that had enabled George Floyd's death turned to our own milieu here in Britain, something vital seemed to get lost in translation. 'People are appalled at racial injustice in America, but refuse to believe the depth of our own problems,' the writer Bernardine Evaristo diagnosed.[2] There is a tendency in Britain to downplay racism in this country by positioning us in relation to the USA, where the racism is often so much more visually spectacular, courtesy of the Ku Klux Klan and the pageantry of those white robes, descriptions of lynchings where men rot like fruit under trees, photographs of the snarling police dogs at Birmingham, and the steady stream of viral moments provided by trigger-happy police officers. Slavery's legacy looms larger in America too, perhaps because individual Americans are themselves living statues memorialising it, as the poet Caroline Randall Williams wrote in the *New York Times*, describing her 'rape-colored skin' as being a monument to the legacy of the Confederacy, 'a living testament' to the white slave-owning ancestors who had raped her enslaved Black ones.[3]

These distinctly American images are what dominate the popular conception of racism, allowing Britain to position itself as the kinder, more progressive, all-round *nicer* relation to its delinquent American cousin – as though Britain itself had not played an essential role in the trans-atlantic slave trade, did not profit enormously from the practice of treating Black people as chattel, had not until 2015 been siphoning off taxpayers' money to compensate formerly slave-owning families for the loss of income they incurred when slavery was abolished.[4]

When in June thousands of far-right protestors descended on London to rally against the
Black Lives Matter movement and the removal
of various relics of Empire, clashing with police
officers and eventually erupting in an explosion
of violence, a prominent Labour MP advised
that we remember these scenes 'do not repre-
sent our country', as though they were not in
fact happening in our country. Weeks later the
leader of the Labour Party would be at pains to
separate the aims of the now global Black Lives
Matter movement from criticisms of the UK's
own police force, confining Black Lives Matter
to 'what happened in America' (that is, George
Floyd's killing). That these were the reactions
from the political left is perhaps enough of an
indicator of those from the right.

There is an idea in Britain that racism here
is an aberration, or the work of a rogue fac-
tion, when in reality it is part of this country's

DNA, the system merely working as designed. At times I detected in the passion and intensity with which white Brits reacted to George Floyd's death, and their horror at the barbarism of American-style racism – dazzling, in-your-face, flagrantly violent, often armed – outrage worn as a comforter, even a sense of relief. *Well at least we're not* that *bad*. A case of the relative being confused with the absolute.

That collective self-delusion and the myth of well-mannered 'British civility' has been startlingly effective propaganda. Years ago, standing on a lively street corner in the middle of a sticky New York summer, a stranger, a Black American man, sidled over to me to try his luck. Upon hearing my accent though (which I'd judiciously pitched at Queen's English levels, having observed how that ingratiated me to most New Yorkers) he immediately changed tack.

'Oh you're from *England*? What's it like over there? I heard it's not as racist as it is here,' he asked, only half-joking.

I hesitated. How to sum up the vagaries of British racism in just a few sentences!

'Mmm . . . I don't think it's better or worse than it is over here. It's just . . . I don't know. Different, I guess.'

How quickly attempted flirtation had turned to political enquiry. *What are your whites like*, he seemed to be asking me. I didn't have the heart to disappoint him by saying *the same as yours*.

A new phenomenon emerged after George Floyd, that of the anti-racism reading list: compilations of books and authors and media intended to serve as guides for white people wanting to educate themselves about anti-Black racism. Spanning genre and form and era, I understood both the logic and the appeal. There is a belief in some quarters that racism is simply a matter of ignorance, and that everyone can therefore be educated out of it (which I suppose is easier to stomach than the idea that racism might be something more conscious, or deliberate). And so the work of the anti-racism reading list begins, like a counter-missionary attempting to decolonise what was previously colonised.

There is of course much to be gained from white people more fully understanding the history and intricacies and complex topography of racism, but I often worry that the exercise of anti-racism reading encourages white people to satisfy – even exhaust – themselves with swotting up on the semantics of the struggle, without necessarily translating that knowledge into real-world action. It's relatively easy to be a theoretical anti-racist. Writing for *The Atlantic*, Saida Grundy observes that consciousness-raising through anti-racist reading often constitutes 'mere filibustering – white people learning about their privilege and power without ever having to sacrifice either', that it can actually undermine progress 'by presenting increased knowledge as the balm for centuries of abuse', and that 'literature and dialogue cannot supplant restorative social policies and laws, organisational change, and structural redress.'[5]

In presenting these lists as the solution to racism, there is a danger that an academic understanding of racism becomes *the* end goal, rather than anything more substantive or action-focused. At my most cynical I wonder if these books are merely training white people not to say out loud the things that they're actually thinking, not that I'm ungrateful for that progression.

Then there is the fact that these lists reduce books written by Black people to mere educational resource or instructional guide, ignoring their literary value and their authors' epistolary achievements. They become medicinal, the implication that anti-racism reading list stalwarts like Toni Morrison or Audre Lorde or Ta-Nehisi Coates might be appreciated first and foremost as a tonic to be choked down in pursuit of racial enlightenment. The value of writing by Black authors becomes determined by its ability to be of service to white people,

Black writers assigned the position of race edu-
cator whether they like it or not. To be clear,
some of the books on these lists *are* intended
as educational tools and written specifically for
that purpose, but many – the vast majority – are
not, though that is how many people will now
come to them. These are the books that you will
hear described as 'vital' or 'important' or – critics' choice – 'necessary' by those who 'don't seem
to know how to engage with work from mar-
ginalised writers beyond stressing that it should
exist',[6] as writer Khanya Khondlo Mtshali puts
it. By virtue of my being Black I found my own
book (*Little Black Book: A Toolkit For Working
Women*) on some of these lists, even though it
doesn't discuss race at all. Part of me wondered
whether people had simply seen the word 'black'
in its title and assumed the obvious.

Still, perhaps better to have your work re-
cast as anti-racist resource rather than your

entire personhood. Occasionally I found myself added to the social media version of these roundups with no mention of my actual work, which I took to mean that my entire life might be considered an 'anti-racist reading list', existing solely to facilitate white people's moment of moral awakening. I flinched at the thought of some hopeful voyeur observing my day-to-day life – photos of the food I was eating, or my thoughts on a movie I'd seen – and considering that to be part of their anti-racist training. At first I tried to untag myself from these posts, in a few cases requesting that they be removed entirely, having also been around the social media block enough times to realise that a sudden influx of attention from uninformed white people is rarely a good thing. But after a few days I gave up. Better to let it wash over me, I decided, than to work myself up playing social media whack-a-mole.

Social media is, unsurprisingly, the site of considerable absurdity during this period, as people rush to post something – anything – for fear that they'll otherwise appear indifferent, although I detect something else in the deluge of broadcasts that emerges too: a need for connection after months of isolation. Without fresh evidence of our daily lives to share on social media, we have all been short of ways to remind the outside world that we still exist, and much of what I see seems to double as a way of proving the fact of that existence to others, a way of saying 'Hey! Don't forget me! I'm still here!' And even though Black and white people are often posting the same images and words, I register the meaning behind them entirely

27

differently depending on who has posted them. There is a difference between talking about white supremacy when you are *of* it, rather than oppressed by it.

The self-reflexive nature of much of this activity is, I think, often reflected in the content that ensues. An influencer with nearly a million followers shares an image to her Instagram page, Black hands intertwined with white ones, before her output returns to the usual fare of handbags and holidays. The Black hands in the photo she has chosen are the darkest shade possible, blue-black skin, underscoring her point with all the subtlety of a hammer (though we are largely left to infer her point, given that the only caption she can muster is a black heart emoji). Meanwhile a white Upper West Side-dwelling writer I follow posts a photo of a Black protestor wiping his friend's tears away with the sleeve of his jumper, captioning the photo 'heartbreaking and beautiful'. *What is beautiful about this*, I want to comment underneath, but I don't. Over and over again that word comes up, describing words, statements, photos, intentions. 'Beautiful.' 'So beautiful.' 'Beautiful!' Each time I wonder *what is 'beautiful' about this moment, about any of this?* I have never in my life seen so much Black pain. Their posts are symptomatic of an inclination towards the romanticisation of the Black struggle I observe many white people exhibit during this period, a need to somehow make this situation aesthetically pleasing. They share creatively sourced imagery – pop-y illustrations and carefully art-directed photos, slick infographics designed to be easily digested and re-shared – and I wonder if the only way they can process this moment is to look at it sidelong, laundering it through the softening lens of an Instagram filter so that it is marginally less grotesque.

The language of activist movements and academia makes its way into the mainstream only to be distorted and misapplied, and certain slogans become the approved mode of expression for any and all anti-racist sentiment, used over and over again until they are devoid of weight, a way to signal introspection even in the clear absence of it. 'It's time for change.' 'We see you.' 'I am muted.' 'Diversify your feed.' There are repeated calls to 'amplify melanated voices', a phrase that sets my teeth on edge every time I see it, which is often. *How does one* melanate *their voice?* I text my Black friends, and we cackle at the absurdity of the phrase, how it strains for profundity while somehow managing to be anything but.

Corporations and the individuals leading them rush to issue bland statements affirming their commitment to diversity, and later on, apologies. Brands scramble to post photos of

Black people, many for the very first time. All of it has the air of panicked damage control, and occasionally, marketing. They are careful to use the black version of the heart emoji as much as possible, which is fine, if a little corny. They mostly seem unaware that this is a private code Black people have been using on social media for years, as a symbol of solidarity, or kinship, or acknowledgement.

People post those infamous black squares.

Everywhere I look white people are thanking each other for taking a stance against racism, desperate to prove that they're 'one of the good ones', and where better to do so than on social media, our modern-day town square. They'd been doing this since even before George Floyd was killed, occasionally turning on themselves where necessary. Early on in the pandemic I watch a white writer being torn apart online for comments deemed to be racist, or at least racially motivated (comments that I myself find to be inoffensive, if slightly caustic). Some of her most vocal critics are other white people, eager to demonstrate their own lack of racism by positioning themselves against hers. This is when you will find white people talking about 'white people' in that strange way they sometimes do, selectively distancing themselves from their kinfolk, or white women moaning about 'old white guys' and playing up their lack of privilege in relation to them, as if to make up for the surplus of it that they are afforded by whiteness, specifically white femininity.

I spend the first few weeks after George Floyd's murder glued to the Internet, compulsively tapping, clicking, refreshing, consuming. I feel compelled by the sense that I am living through history to *see* everything, to take it all in and document it for posterity. At one point the app that routinely torments me by tracking how much time I spend on my phone informs me that I have racked up nearly fourteen hours in a single day, so I decide to stop checking it as often (the app, not my phone).

Most shocking to me is how clearly the impact of those weeks affects my physical health. My muscles ache constantly, inexplicably so, and after a particularly intense few days I become aware of my heart beating unusually hard in my chest. My appetite, usually reliably insatiable, disappears, and at one point I am averaging only three hours' sleep a night. (These latter two things are particularly surprising to me because even at my lowest points, two things generally remain unchanged: that I can eat, and I can sleep.) I find it impossible to work, unable to centre my thoughts for more than a few minutes at a time, and the book I am supposed to be writing goes unattended for weeks.

I am also the most consistently angry I have ever been, so angry that sometimes I can feel myself literally *vibrating* with rage. My body is full to the brim with it. At times like this, when racism is 'in the air', it's impossible not to think about all the ways, known and unknown, that it has held you back in life. It's not as if I don't already think about those things, but at least most of the time it's not a constant thought filling my every waking hour, not like now. 'Weathering' is the sociological term used to describe how the chronic stress of constant exposure to racism negatively impacts Black people's health. I had long been aware of the term in an academic sense, but it takes on new significance now that I can physically feel it happening to me, the constant thinking and talking about racism draining my health day by day.

White people are eroding my body.

A problem: some of my best friends are white.

After the 2019 general election, I am devastated. Even though I'd anticipated the overall outcome, the sheer scale of the Conservative victory still winds me. The fact that even after Grenfell and Windrush and Brexit, and the comments about piccaninnies and letterboxes, people *still* voted for them. It feels like a covert referendum on people like me and our right to be here (or 'right to remain', to use the official term). Immigrants. Black. Brown. People who buy Scotch bonnets by the pound and gripe about the rising cost of plantain. For the first time in my life I am nervous about renewing my British passport, which expired a few days before the election; even more so when I find out that a friend's mother is having trouble renewing hers. She has lived in this country longer than I have been alive. The hostile environment feels especially hostile.

None of my white friends know to ask how I am.

I am supposed to be attending a friend's Christmas party the following night but I cancel at the last minute, because I know I'll probably be the only Black person in a room full of white ones. I'm worried that after the requisite hand-wringing about the election results, someone will blithely suggest we talk about something less depressing 'because it's Christmas', and I will smash a plate against a wall because I don't think there's anything else we should be talking about, don't think it's fair that white people get to change the subject. So instead I stay home and cry.

George Floyd is killed, and this time my

white friends know to ask how I am, if only because the Internet has told them to. There is a tidal wave of texts and calls and emails, and suddenly friends and acquaintances and even total strangers who have never before engaged me on the subject of racism are reaching out in their droves. My inbox becomes a dumping ground for white guilt, for people to demonstrate that they are either 'doing the work' or planning to do the work, and even though I can sense that they're looking for validation I resist the impulse to offer any praise or thank yous. Occasionally I wonder how many of the people reaching out to check that I'm okay are reaching out to the white people in their lives to check if they too are 'okay'. Replying to all these messages stretches my abilities as a writer and I try my best to formulate responses that are honest without being overly harsh, but by the eighth or ninth vague '*how are you?*' text, my patience has run out. I respond with a curt but polite message explaining simply that I have 'run out of capacity for white guilt', adding an 'x' to the end to soften the words. I don't get a reply. A month later that friend calls me at 1 a.m. to apologise. I am asleep.

Everywhere white shame looms large, sucking the oxygen out of the room, threatening to obscure the issue at hand. Even at their most penitent, white people have a way of making it hard to breathe.

After George Floyd is killed, I am determined not to prioritise white comfort over the truth, not to allow for the disconnect between internal monologue and outward display that often arises when I engage with white people on race. This resolve is a fairly recent development, a departure from decades of treading delicately around white people's feelings, having observed that life is generally easier if you avoid disturbing white people's perceptions of themselves as progressive and right-on.

Here are some things I've learned:

- That white people are generally happy to acknowledge racism, just so long as they don't feel that they themselves are being accused of it. Racism is the preserve of 'other' white people, the bad ones.

- When discussing racism with white people, make it clear that you don't see them as one of *those* white people, even if they are, and even if you do. In moments like this it's best to speak in vaguer terms, about 'structural' racism or 'implicit bias', to avoid anyone feeling too attacked.

- When a white person tells you in shocked tones about a situation where they witnessed someone acting in a racist manner, you do not ask why this white person did not themselves challenge this behaviour, because that's not why they're telling you the story. They're telling you because they want *you* to know, that *they* know, that racism is wrong.

A memory:

It's Friday night and I'm at home getting ready to go meet my friends Molly and Amelia for a celebratory drink. Molly has just passed her driving test. As the three of us ping messages back and forth, it transpires that some of Molly's friends from work will also be joining us. My heart sinks. I've never actually met her colleagues before, but she works at a creative agency in east London, so I know pretty much what to expect, having myself once worked at a creative agency in east London: white people who consider themselves socially progressive because they have mildly countercultural tastes and have been to G-A-Y a few times.

'For people of colour, some aspect of friendship with white people involves an awareness that you could be dropped through a trapdoor of racism at any moment, by a slip of the tongue, or at a campus party, or in a legislative campaign. But it's not always anticipated.'[7] These are the words of the journalist Wesley Morris, which to me feel like the truest description of the Black experience when navigating white spaces (although I personally would extend his definition beyond the boundaries of just friendship and apply it to 'being around white people' in general). The older I get, the more on edge I feel in these sorts of situations, having learned that a slip of the tongue is never that far away, no matter how progressive the company.

At the pub now, I'm queuing to buy a drink, ending up in conversation with Molly's boss while we're both waiting to be served.

I'd been on a shoot run by a Swedish production crew a few days earlier and in telling him about it I make the obvious joke, about how good-looking Swedish people are, especially in comparison to us trollish, sun-starved and rain-soaked Brits.

'Yeah, I know,' he replies, continuing, 'and they're all beautiful in that really, like, *Aryan*-looking way as well,' as though dreamily invoking a beauty standard popularised by a regime that murdered six million Jews in part because they didn't conform to it is an entirely normal thing to say. I am lost for words, and the conversation moves on while I'm still processing his comment.

Later that evening, I am in conversation with another of Molly's colleagues, who proceeds to tell me in far too much detail about a messy break up he's just been through, and the ex-girlfriend who is now dragging her feet over repaying him the £20,000 he (foolishly, in my opinion) lent her. I ask lots of questions, polite but ultimately bemused, and we speculate about the potential legal recourse he might be able to take.

'She's also half Jamaican, half Guyanese,' he comments, before moving on to another detail of what is becoming clear is an incredibly bizarre situation.

'Wait, what? I don't understand,' I say, the back of my neck suddenly hot and tight. I know where this is headed, and that I should spare myself the discomfort, but I prod him anyway.

'What?' he replies.

'You just mentioned that she's half Jamaican, half Guyanese. I don't understand. How is that relevant?' I say neutrally, feigning confusion.

'Oh just . . .' he tails off, trying to change the subject, but I press.

'Well I'm like, from the countryside,' he elaborates, a non sequitur if ever I heard one. 'I'd literally never met a Black person before I moved to London. I didn't know *any* Black people.'

'Right . . .' I say blankly. 'I still don't get it,' even though I do, but I want him to say plainly what he had only been brave enough to insinuate.

'Oh nothing,' he says. 'I just learned a lot from the situation, that's all.'

'Like what?'

'Just not to trust people, y'know?'

'Black people?'

'No! No, no, no, no. That's not what I meant. I don't know why I brought up her race, it's not relevant.'

I give him an icy smile and abruptly end the conversation, turning to speak to someone else, and he leaves almost immediately after, avoiding my gaze as he waves goodbye to the table. I am reminded that no matter how carefully I choose my own friends, I cannot control for or vet the white people they bring into my life.

The next day I go to a Black friend's birthday party, and I am pathetically grateful for its timing, and to be surrounded by other Black people, Black joy, Black children, Black food. It feels almost baptismal, like I am being washed clean of what happened the night before.

There are other examples, too many to count or remember. Here are a few:

During freshers' week I am at one of the many cheesy, drunken nights of organised fun that define the British university experience. On this particular night we have been instructed to dress up in school uniform, which seems like an odd and fairly unimaginative choice of fancy dress to impose on a group of people who not that long ago had no choice but to wear school uniforms. I am standing in a corner with a newly acquired friend, the two of us quietly entertaining ourselves by taking it in turns to gently mock others' efforts on the dance floor, when out of the blue he turns to me and jokes, 'oh, you're just jealous of them because you're not *white*!' It is as shocking as a punch, and my enthusiasm for the party evaporates instantly. Not long after, I leave and go to bed, lying awake and wondering if I've made a mistake in coming to Oxford.

A few weeks later I am at a house party and, feeling bold, decide to commandeer the sound system, putting on a rap album I've been listening to on repeat. O.D.B. comes blaring out of the speakers and almost immediately one of the second years (whose house it is) drunkenly yells at me to play something else, telling me my music is 'too Black'. I am mortified and do as instructed, cowed.

Another time, a boy in my year group confidently informs me that he doesn't know any Nigerians who were educated at Harrow (specifically, Harrow) whose parents weren't in some way 'involved in corruption'. Irritated, I ask him for proof, though of course he has none, just thought it would be a funny thing to say.

On to the workplace now: I am gossiping with a few of my colleagues at the ad agency where I work, crowded around a colleague's phone as we take in the latest innovation wrought by the smartphone age – a dating app, the first of many to come. We are collectively sizing up the app's offerings, rapid-fire scrolling through the motley crew of bachelors presented to us, dismissing the keen and mocking the deluded, the topless, the desperate, the inarticulate and the crude. *Yes, no, yes, no, no, no, no*. At one point she swipes *yes* on a potential suitor and another colleague interjects, confused: 'I thought you said you weren't into Black guys!' presumably referencing a previous, private conversation. The swiper turns red and protests unconvincingly, quickly moving the conversation on to something else. She at least has the good grace to look embarrassed, whereas the colleague who'd exposed her witters on, seemingly oblivious to the impact of her words. I feel the tenor of the group shift imperceptibly and pretend I have a meeting to go to.

Every time the trapdoor opens, the physical sensation is the same: your stomach lurches the way it does when you're on a roller coaster that has just begun its descent and you are momentarily weightless, your stomach separated from the rest of your body, travelling a few seconds behind. A hot flash at the back of your neck begins creeping up towards your ears. Involuntarily, almost instinctively, you become focused on making your face appear as neutral as possible to cover up your embarrassment, decades of practice having hardened into a reflex (and it is always you that feels embarrassed, never your assailant).

Even after all these years, the descent still comes as a surprise.

The question that for me rather unexpectedly emerged from the aftermath of George Floyd's murder, was whether white allyship as a concept truly exists, whether it *can* exist. I say 'unexpectedly' because if one wanted to debate the existence of white allyship, there really would be no greater proof of concept than this past summer. And yet I found myself wondering.

In order to appreciate the discussion of allyship that follows, it's necessary to understand two things about whiteness, the first being that it is a social construct: an assumed and assigned identity defined by the aggregation of various rights, benefits and social status accruing to those who are deemed 'white' (which is itself a category that has historically changed over time. The Irish, Italians, and Jewish people have not always been considered 'white' or enjoyed the attendant benefits, having alternately faced discrimination and persecution because of perceived racial difference. Many Jewish people today still do not consider themselves to be 'white').

By whiteness I don't mean the property of having white (i.e. pale) skin, but rather the *system* of whiteness, which as scholars from W. E. B. Du Bois through to James Baldwin and Robin DiAngelo have noted, is dependent for its existence – and its supremacy – on the imagined inferiority of Blackness, and the exclusion and subjugation of a non-white 'other'; what Toni Morrison called 'the sycophancy of white identity'.[8]

Second, understand that whiteness does not see itself. It is positioned as the default, the norm from which everything else deviates. From this vantage point, whites look out and survey others, but not themselves. Toni Morrison again, in discussing the American literary tradition, notes that white authors frequently imagine themselves to be 'unraced', even as they inhabit 'the wholly racialised society that is the United States'.[9] Whiteness is usually rendered invisible, though as the academic Sara Ahmed writes, '[it] is only invisible for those who inhabit it. For those who don't, it is hard not to see whiteness; it even seems everywhere.'[10]

Recently white people have begun to see themselves.

A week after George Floyd was killed, the *New York Times* published an op-ed that argued for the use of military force against Black Lives Matter protestors ('an overwhelming show of force'),[11] the Republican senator who'd written the piece essentially encouraging violence from one agent of the state to solve a crisis that had been wrought by the violence of another. Backlash to the article was both immediate and severe, aimed not just at the author's dangerous and plainly anti-democratic suggestions, but also at the editorial decision to give them a wider platform, lending both author and argument the sheen of credibility by publishing them in the paper of record.

And it was at this precise moment that I began to doubt the depth of white commitments to allyship, and to question even its conceptual possibility – because despite what I understood to be cross-racial agreement among the *New York Times'* more progressive-minded staff that the decision to publish this op-ed had been unconscionable, it was the paper's few Black journalists who were first to publicly and explicitly condemn it (defying the *New*

York Times' employee social media policy, and thereby risking their jobs). Their white colleagues followed suit, eventually, but the order of play left an indelible impression – that when push comes to shove even the most high-minded white progressives often aren't willing to enact the self-sacrifice that true allyship requires. That this had happened even as discussions of racial injustice and the necessity of white allyship were at an all-time high left me even more disturbed. What would happen when the news cycle moved on and white people no longer felt themselves to be under a magnifying glass? *We're all we've got*, I found myself thinking, and the thought lingered in my mind for days.

That episode was one of many in recent months that illustrated something I'd observed long before I ever even heard George Floyd's name – that although many white people really do feel deep moral concern over racial injustice, they baulk at what undoing that necessarily entails, because it is often difficult, personally taxing, and highly inconvenient. Real allyship requires white people to put themselves on the line for Black people without the promise of getting anything *back* (besides perhaps, moral satisfaction), and the denouement of the *New York Times* story demonstrated to me both the magnitude and the improbability of that ask. I began to wonder whether mere moral concern is enough of a motivator for white people, when it is not their lives or their livelihoods or their freedom that's at stake, when they quite literally don't have skin in the game.

At my most generous, I put the gap between alleged intent and actual action down to a misunderstanding. The mainstream conception of allyship popularised by the Internet and in the plethora of increasingly pandering allyship handbooks now springing up has, perhaps inevitably, been watered down in the interests of accessibility. It tends to consist of variations on the following themes: that white people should use their privilege and access to advocate for and defend Black people; that they should call out racial injustice wherever they see it; that they should listen to Black people and amplify our voices; that they should educate themselves and others about racism, and so on. And certainly these are things that white people absolutely should be doing, but they are also in the grand scheme of things, wildly insufficient. Like the anti-racism reading list, this definition of allyship allows white people to feel as though they have done something significant, often while only doing the bare minimum. A perfect example of this is the emphasis on the importance of 'checking one's privilege', which almost always crops up in discussions of allyship. Increasingly, acknowledgement of one's privilege (white or otherwise) is a hastily added caveat to the narration of one's experiences or achievements, its purpose to make clear to others that you are at least *aware* of the unfair advantages you've been granted by virtue of skin colour, class background, gender, or whatever your own particular stroke of luck. Conveying that self-awareness becomes an end in itself, a moral get-out clause alleviating the pressure to do anything more substantial to offset that privilege.

But racism is so all-encompassing, so deeply rooted, so goddamn *big*, for lack of a better word. It seems obvious to me that it can't and won't be undone by white people performing these relatively modest actions, that to dismantle something of that magnitude requires opposing actions of a similar scale.

In 1993 the activist and historian Noel Ignatiev, as part of a lifelong commitment to labour activism and overturning white supremacy, began with some others to publish a journal called *Race Traitor*. By Ignatiev's definition, 'race traitors' are those white people fully committed to the abolition of whiteness, a category in which he included himself, as a white American of Jewish descent. Exploring the rationale and means by which whiteness might be abolished was the journal's driving purpose, and its motto – 'treason to whiteness is loyalty to humanity' – positioned white people's renunciation of whiteness as a moral imperative. Similarly the writer Eula Biss, also white, describes whiteness not as an identity, but as 'a moral problem', though she notes that refusing to collude in injustice as a white person is far easier said than done: 'Collusion is written onto our way of life, and nearly every interaction among white people is an invitation to collusion.'[12]

Recently I discovered the academic Barnor Hesse's *The 8 White Identities*, which he describes as 'an ethnography of whiteness', and which I've found to be a useful framework for understanding how committed (or not) individual white people are to overthrowing whiteness. It starts at (1) 'white supremacy', which Hesse defines as those who preserve, name and value white superiority – these are your far-right protestors, your Ku Klux Klans. At (4) and (5) are 'white benefit' and 'white confessional', which to my eye is where most white progressives are situated: 'sympathetic to a set of issues but only privately. Will not speak/act in solidarity publicly, because they are benefitting through whiteness in public', and slightly more helpfully, 'some exposure of whiteness takes place' (this latter definition is that of the 'white confessional'). But where things really get interesting – and what I believe true allyship looks like – is at the furthest ends of the scale, at (7) 'white traitor', defined by Hesse as the white person who 'actively refuses complicity; names what's going on; intention is to subvert white authority and tell the truth at whatever cost', and (8) the 'white abolition-ist', who 'changes institutions; dismantling whiteness, and not allowing whiteness to re-assert itself'. It's these two considerably more radical categorisations and the power they hold for real transformation that to me constitute true allyship – but too many would-be allies are clustered around 'white confessional' (and believe that is sufficient both to constitute ally-ship, and to end racial injustice). This is not to dismiss their efforts – 'white confessional' is of course better than nothing – but it's also time to acknowledge that those efforts aren't going to get us where we need to go.

I know it will have offended some people to read the words 'abolish whiteness' over and over again, and that such a statement might be interpreted as a desire to abolish white people or something similarly genocidal, which of course it isn't (and that would be an unforgivable sentiment either to feel, or express). Noel Ignatiev himself offered up the following useful analogy as clarification, comparing the abolition of whiteness to anti-monarchism: 'to oppose monarchy does not mean killing the king; it means getting rid of crowns, thrones, royal titles, etc.'[13]

I would love at this point to grandstand and say something pithy and quotable about how power is not given but taken, but I suspect that white supremacy is too far gone, too powerful, and too deeply entrenched for it to be overthrown without what amounts to inside help. It enjoys an incumbent's advantage that spans centuries, impressive in its ability to absorb, neutralise and then punish threats to its dominance. A Black American president is elected, upsetting the status quo, and at the next available opportunity those who are offended by that fact vote to replace him with an unashamed racist.

Black people cannot ourselves abolish whiteness – white people will need to relinquish it. Allyship, almost by definition, involves actively divesting from the structures that oppress Black people and unfairly elevate white ones. It is the surrendering of racialised privileges, the turning down of the advantages your skin colour affords you. In the moment that white privilege offers itself up to you, can you – *will* you – say 'no'? Will you start boycotting the hairdresser who gives you an amazing blow-dry but who you know doesn't cut Afro hair; or the make-up brand that sells the best foundation you've ever tried, but doesn't cater to Black skin? Will you say something when your boss makes a loaded comment about Black people, potentially risking your own employment, or will you squirm uncomfortably in your seat and bitch about it to your friends after work instead? What will you do when you find out that the Black colleague who does the same job as you is being paid far less than you are – or will it just be their problem to figure out? Consider that (depending on your gender, specific trade, and a few other variables) you are paid perhaps 10 or 20 or even 30 per cent more to work, simply because you are white. What to do with those ill-gotten gains? Keep them?

White privilege is an exceedingly comfortable perch to occupy, at least from what I can gather. To give it up will be as materially inconvenient and difficult for white people as that privilege currently is for Black people. Either white people don't yet understand that, or they know it but are not willing to do so – and so we are left with actions like 'amplifying Black voices', or 'advocating for the Black community', which although helpful are not fundamentally redistributive or disruptive to the status quo.

How to tell white people that going on marches, patronising Black-owned businesses, reading Black writers, and amplifying our voices – that all of that is not enough? That if they take allyship seriously, they stand to lose the privileges that are as integral to their lives as breathing. That losing those privileges is necessary. That allyship will cost them the shape of their lives as they know it. That I do not think they are willing to pay that price.

ENDNOTES

1 Noor Brara, 'Nine Black Artists and Cultural Leaders on Seeing and Being Seen', *New York Times Style Magazine*, 24 June 2020.

2 Bernardine Evaristo, 'Why Black Lives Matter', *A Point of View*, BBC Radio 4, 3 July 2020.

3 Caroline Randall Williams, 'My Body Is a Confederate Monument', *New York Times*, 26 June 2020.

4 David Olusoga, 'The Treasury's tweet shows slavery is still misunderstood', *The Guardian*, 12 February 2018.

5 Saida Grundy, 'The False Promise of Anti-Racism Books', *The Atlantic*, 21 July 2020.

6 Khanya Khondlo Mtshali, 'The Black Girl Looks at Other Black Girls', *LA Review of Books*, 24 July 2018.

7 Wesley Morris, 'Dumber Than Your Average Bear', *Grantland*, 24 June 2015.

8   Toni Morrison, *Playing In The Dark*, Vintage, 1992.

9   Ibid.

10 Sara Ahmed, *Declarations of Whiteness: The Non-Performativity of Anti-Racism*, borderlands, 3(2).

11 Tom Cotton, 'Send In the Troops', *New York Times*, 3 June 2020.

12 Eula Biss, 'White Debt', *New York Times*, 2 December 2015.

13 Excerpted from *When Race Becomes Real: Black and White Writers Confront Their Personal Histories*, edited by Bernestine Singley, Lawrence Hill Books, 2002.

ACKNOWLEDGEMENTS

To my agent Emma Paterson – thank you for not letting me back out of writing this, and for persuading me to at least try.

To my editor Michelle Kane – thank you for always having such total faith in my ideas, and for allowing me the creative freedom (read: control) that you do.

Thank you to all at 4th Estate for the care with which you publish my work, and for always allowing me nuance.

Thank you to Reni Eddo-Lodge for reading an early draft of this essay, and for your honest critique (now and always!).

ACKNOWLEDGEMENTS

Thank you to the community of Black friends and peers around me, especially the women, for being a vital outlet, support network and constant sounding board. The WhatsApps say it all.

With thanks to The Heart's *Race Traitor* podcast series for introducing me to the concept.

NOTE ON THE AUTHOR

OTEGHA UWAGBA is the author of *Sunday Times* bestseller *Little Black Book: A Toolkit for Working Women* (2017). Her writing has been published in the *Guardian*, *The Cut*, *i-D* and *Dazed*, among other publications, and she was selected for the Forbes 30 Under 30 Media list in 2018. She graduated with a degree in PPE from Oxford, and grew up in South London, where she still resides.